The
Magic
of the
Medals

Kim D. Fellwock

ISBN Number:
0-9650432-0-7

KatMar Publishing, Inc.
Brentwood, Tennessee

The Magic of the Medals

100 Insightful Quotes from Olympic Athletes
100 Exciting Thoughts Worthy of a Gold Medal
100 Powerful Phrases with a Silver Lining
100 Motivational Idioms That Should Be in Bronze
100% Inspiration for Success Today

Special thanks to

Getting The Edge Company
230 Huron Road N.W., Suite 85-83
Cleveland, Ohio 44113
(800) 452-3343

Various quotes from Olympic athletes were
obtained from the motivational book

The Edge:
The Guide to Fulfilling Dreams,
Maximizing Success
and Enjoying a Lifetime of
Achievement

by
Howard E. Ferguson

Contents

Discover the Winning Spirit

The Purpose...

This book is not about the Olympic Games where athletes run, jump, swim, kayak, or wrestle. This book is about the Olympic spirit that is stated in the Olympic Creed:

> "The most important thing in the Olympic Games is not to win but to take part, just as the most important thing in life is not the triumph but the struggle. The essential thing is not to have conquered, but to have fought well."

The Olympic spirit is a winning spirit. A winning spirit is the answer to the question, "What is the 'magic' of the medals?"

The winning spirit embraces the concept of "taking part" and "fighting well." To take part means stepping outside your comfort zone and taking risks to achieve your potential. To have fought well means defeating your self-doubts and fears, making the best of where you are, accepting responsibility and moving forward. This is the spirit that the book captures.

The inspirational thoughts in this book—from Olympic athletes and others who understand the importance of "taking part" and "fighting well"—will challenge you to discover the winning spirit within yourself and motivate you to live life to its fullest.

How the Book Came About...

The idea to write about discovering this magic spirit within all of us began while I was in college. During my freshman year, my school went to the National Collegiate Athletic Association (NCAA) basketball finals. The school spirit that surrounded that event was exciting, contagious and so positive you could almost hold it in the palm of your hand. I realized then how real the aura around spirit was and what a positive impact it could have.

During college, I had several classes in a building with a small monument outside the front entrance. On the monument was a plaque stating the school's motto:

THE SPIRIT MAKES THE MASTER

As I walked to and from classes, I paused and read that motto many times. It had a special meaning to me. One day, I even went to the school bookstore with the sole purpose of purchasing a university notebook that had that motto on the front cover. Twenty years later, I still have that notebook.

Through the years I have remained aware of the special magic of spirit. I have seen it overflow from people in our church, and witnessed community spirit rise because of a special occasion or festival. A caring spirit has often prevailed in companies where I have worked when a co-worker needed help. People show spirit in a number of different and exciting ways.

I recently traveled through the Atlanta airport. All the terminals featured posters and pictures announcing the coming of the Olympic Games. Without diminishing the importance of spirit at school, church, community or work, the spirit that surrounds the Olympic Games has always intrigued me. A person can watch the Olympics and see the winning spirit in action. This spirit is in the athletes who prepare, challenge, persist, concentrate, hope, learn, risk, dream, excel, win and enjoy. This is the spirit we need in our lives today, and I decided to learn more about it.

To learn more about the spirit that surrounds the Olympics, I drove to the main branch of the Nashville Public Library. I wanted to find all of the books that had been written on the spirit of the Olympics. Using the library's sophisticated computer system, I typed in the words *olympic* and *spirit*. The computer screen quickly indicated that there were 130 books in print that contained the word *olympic* in the title. The screen also showed that the word *spirit* was in 447 titles.

However, not one book in print today focused on the unique winning spirit to take part and fight well. At that moment, I resolved to change that.

An Olympian with Spirit...

In 1895, when Jim Connolly was a Harvard University student, an advertisement in a magazine caught his attention. It was an announcement that the Olympic Games were being revived the following year in Athens, Greece. They had not been held since 393 A.D. Jim, who excelled at the hop, step and jump, requested a leave of absence from Harvard to compete in the Olympics. The university denied the request. Determined to compete, Jim dropped out of school. He requested financial assistance from several organizations to help defer the cost to Athens. When no one donated, he paid his own way.

He sailed from New York on March 20, 1896, on an ocean steamer not designed to accommodate passengers. There was no place on the steamer to exercise. The ship reached Naples, Italy on April 1, and there he learned that the Greek calendar differed from the American calendar by a few days. The Olympic games were actually scheduled to begin on April 6, not April 18, as he had thought.

The only way to get from Naples to Athens involved another cramped boat trip, this time to Patras, Greece. He arrived in Patras on the evening of April 5, with only 10 hours left to reach Athens for the start of the Olympic Games. He endured yet another trip, this time a rough train ride from Patras to Athens. He arrived at the Olympic stadium as the announcer was calling the first events. He quickly found his way to the hop, step and jump event. The event coordinator asked who he was.

Jim offered no excuses about Harvard's refusal to grant his leave, his unsuccessful attempt to find sponsors, his long and uncomfortable trip, the differences between the Greek and U.S. calendars, his inability to exercise during his travels or the fact that he had just arrived at the stadium. He simply answered, "Connolly of the United States."

Jim Connolly won the first gold medal awarded at Olympic competition in 1,503 years. Jim Connolly had the Olympic spirit, the drive to take part and fight well.

How to Experience the Book...

The book is divided into four sections, each designed to help you discover the winning spirit within yourself.

The first section contains 100 inspirational comments from Olympic athletes.

The second section offers thoughts and verses worthy of a gold medal from people who also understand the magic of the spirit.

The third section contains messages with a silver lining about the impact of living life with a positive attitude.

The fourth section is a collection of idioms that should be in bronze and kept in the forefront of your mind.

Twenty-nine times in the book you will see a quote with one particular word in bold type. That word helps to further define the meaning of spirit. The following page has the dictionary definition of that word, which may vary from what you expect. Each word will also have several synonyms listed. The synonyms will help you fully understand the word so you can make it come alive in your life.

We live in a hectic world. It is difficult to find time for all the projects, chores and tasks we face each day. This book is designed to meet your schedule: you can read it all the way through, a section at a time or page by page. Keep it handy, refer back to it and keep your Olympic spirit alive.

100 Insightful Quotes by Olympic Athletes

Although they only give gold medals
in the field of athletics,
I encourage everyone to look into themselves
and find their own personal **dream**,
whatever that may be—
sports, medicine, law, business,
music, writing, whatever.
The same principles apply.
Turn your **dream** into a goal,
and decide how to attack that goal
systematically.
Break it into bite-size chunks
that seem possible—
and then don't give up.
Just keep plugging away.

John Naber
Swimmer

DREAM

Webster's Collegiate Dictionary

Dream:
1. a vision voluntarily indulged in while awake
2. an aspiration
3. an aim
4. a goal
5. to think or conceive of something

The Synonym Finder

Dream: vision, suppose, conceive, think, conjure up, idealize, stargaze, imagine, invention, fantasy, fancy, notion, thought, plan, idea

I have to go all out in every practice. I can't stand the idea of loafing. It's the only way I can swim without consciously getting tired.

Shelley Mann
Swimmer

One of the great lessons I've learned in athletics is that you've got to discipline your life. No matter how good you may be, you've got to be willing to cut out of your life those things that keep you from going to the top.

Bob Richards
Pole Vaulter

I don't think the mile has really been tapped yet. There's still time to come off. But you can only do it by being courageous and going fast at the start.

Sebastian Coe
Distance Runner

I do believe that by providing an example of what can be accomplished if you apply your thoughts and energy with great determination, more people will make the first attempt toward some distant goal.

Al Oerter
Discus Thrower

I had everything to win, but little to lose.

Eric Liddell
200 Meter

The medals don't mean anything
and the glory doesn't last.
It's all about your happiness.

Jackie Joyner Kersee
Pentathlete and Long Jumper

After years of competing and coaching,
I know that every defeat
is a lesson for eventual victory.

Sammy Lee
Diver

I was just thinking one shot at a time. It's
my job to stop the puck and that's what I
do. Just going one shot at a time.

Ray LeBlanc
Hockey Player

Basketball is just
something else to do,
another facet of life.
I'm going to be a
success at whatever
I choose because
of my **preparation**.
By the time the
game starts,
the outcome
is already decided.
I never think about
having a bad game
because I have
prepared.

David Robinson
Basketball Player

PREPARE

Webster's Collegiate Dictionary

Prepare: 1. to put in proper condition
                2. to compose
                3. to put one self in readiness
                4. to make or put together out of parts

The Synonym Finder

Prepare: equip, furnish, provide, fit, make, produce, construct, build, mold, combine, compose, develop, devise, invent, dream up, train, familiarize, rehearse, practice, condition

Even to lose, I think I'd still compete.
No matter how it goes or how I go,
I wouldn't change anything. It fulfills
me to be able to compete.
I never worry about winning or losing
because when you compete,
you are already a winner.

Daley Thompson
Decathlete

I never, never go into a wrestling match
thinking I can get beat.
The thought of losing
never crosses my mind.
There is no reason for me to get beat.
I know that I have more ability than anyone
I wrestle. When I lose it means I didn't
wrestle to my full potential. The solution
to everything is to work harder.

John Smith
Wrestler

When I think about how much work it took
to get here...it's unbelievable.

Brian Ledbetter
Yachtsman

Everyone should have a dream.
Everyone should work toward that dream.

Jesse Owens
100/200 Meter and Long Jumper

Hard work is the answer.
There is no other way.

Matt Biondi
Swimmer

That kind of training meant both quantity
and quality. I would do my routines over and
over again, as many as thirty repeats.
Then, at the end of this four-or-five-hour
workout at the UCLA gym, I would go back
to my club gym and do weight training.
I really pushed myself to the breaking point,
but it did bring its rewards.

Peter Vidmar
Gymnast

I'm not the greatest;
I'm the double greatest.
Not only do I knock'em out,
I pick the round.

Muhammad Ali
Boxer

My **concentration** level
blocks out everything.
Concentration is why
some athletes are
better than others.
You develop that
concentration in training.
You can't be lackadaisical
in training and
concentrate in a meet.

Edwin Moses
Hurdler

CONCENTRATION

Webster's Collegiate Dictionary

Concentration:
1. to bring or draw to a common center or point of union
2. to direct toward one point
3. to intensify
4. to gather all of one's thoughts
5. to make or become stronger

The Synonym Finder

Concentration: gathering, assemblage, cluster, focus, draw together, study, strengthen, intensity, devotion, meditation, deep thought, consideration, press, centrality

Yes, the pain shot through me like a knife.
It brought tears to my eyes. But now I have
a gold medal, and the pain is gone.
(After competing in the Olympics with a broken leg.)

Shun Fujimoto
Gymnast

I wasn't thinking gold or anything.
I was doing what I came to do,
which was to have fun.

Brian Boitano
Figure Skater

I'm convinced I had the performance of my
life. That's what I came here for. I've played
this day out 400 times in my head, and it's
better than I ever imagined.

Kristen Babb-Sprague
Syncronized Swimmer

I have my fun...and I think
I am a better swimmer because of it.

Dawn Fraser
Swimmer

If I work on a certain move constantly, then, finally, it doesn't seem so risky to me. The idea is that the move stays dangerous and it looks dangerous to my foes, but it is not to me. Hard work has made it easy. That is my secret. That is why I win.

Nadia Comaneci
Gymnast

Twenty years from now,
I can look at this medal and say,
"I was the best quarter-miler
in the world on that day."
If you don't think that's important, you don't know what's inside an athlete's soul.

Vince Matthews
Quarter-Miler

If you trust your nerve as well as your skill, you're capable of a lot more than you can imagine. I never felt that if I didn't win the gold medal, I was nothing. I just had to give it my best shot.

Debi Thomas
Figure Skater

If I didn't think I could win,
I wouldn't have entered.

Emil Zatopek
5,000 and 10,000 Meter

The most important thing is
to love your sport.
Never do it to please someone else—
it has to be yours.
That is all that will justify
the hard work needed to achieve success.
Compete against yourself, not others,
for that is who is truly
your best competition.

Peggy Fleming
Figure Skater

I wanted to do something nobody else had
ever done before.... I started training
the very next day.

Pat McCormick
Diver

I'm proud I went for it on the final dive. I knew what I needed and I went for it... it just didn't happen.

Julie Ovenhouse
Diver

There can be no excuses.
You can't say that you didn't like the snow or that you didn't feel in top form.

Jean-Claude Killy
Skier

So many things can be a factor—
the snow, the weather,
is it warm so that waxing is a factor?
Will you fall? Will someone else
just have an incredible run?
All I can do is run my race,
run it the best I can, and we'll see after
everybody gets to the bottom.

Phil Mahre
Skier

I know a lot of people
think it's monotonous,
down the black lines
over and over,
but it's not if you're **enjoying**
what you're doing.

Tracy Caulkins
Swimmer

ENJOY

Webster's Collegiate Dictionary

Enjoy: 1. to experience with joy
              2. to take pleasure in
              3. to have and use with satisfaction
              4. to find or experience pleasure

The Synonym Finder

Enjoy: be pleased, benefit, profit from, delight, relish, pleasure, satisfaction, rejoice, appreciate, have a good time, have a ball, reap, make the most of

I'm trying to do the best I can.
I'm not concerned about tomorrow,
but with what goes on today.

Mark Spitz
Swimmer

Successful weight-lifting is not in the body.
It's in the mind. You can lift as much
as you believe you can.

Tommy Kono
Weight Lifter

Anything good is developed slowly.

Sebastian Coe
Distance Runner

I love to compete, but people don't always
take me seriously. Someone asked me about
a gold medal, that's the only reason I'm here.
I didn't come all the way over here to be in
the Olympics. I don't need a uniform. I'm
here to win. That's all I'm here for.

Herschel Walker
Bobsledder

People ask me what makes a great skier.
It takes the gift; but besides the gift
it takes that availability of mind
which permits total control
of all the elements that lead to victory—
total composure.

Jean-Claude Killy
Skier

I race for fun.
It's not worthwhile unless you enjoy it.

Dave Lawrence
Skier

I emphasize just one thing,
and that is the need for goals.

Willie Davenport
Hurdler

I don't think about the competition.
I only go as fast as I can.
That's it.
The results will come.

Alberto Tomba
Skier

I knew what I had to do,
so I just cut loose.

Andrea Mead Lawrence
Skier

I feel that the most important step in
any major accomplishment is setting a
specific goal. This enables you to keep your
mind focused on your goal and off the
many obstacles that will arise while you're
striving to do your best.

Kurt Thomas
Gymnast

The only way you can win it is by suffering
a lot—by working through the pain.

Eric Heiden
Speed Skater

When I'd get tired and want to stop,
I'd wonder what my next opponent
was doing. I'd wonder if he was still
working out. I tried to visualize him.
When I could see him still working,
I'd start pushing myself.

Dan Gable
Wrestler

Just as it is in life,
the blending of effort and
the proper technique always
produces results.
Success happens whenever
preparation meets opportunity.

John Naber
Swimmer

Once I go around that last turn
into the homestretch in the lead,
nobody is going to beat me.

Herb McKenley
200 Meter

The resources of the human body and soul,
physical, mental and spiritual,
are enormous and beyond our present
knowledge and expectations.
We go part of the way to consciously
tapping these resources by having goals
that we want desperately—
it is the only way we currently know
how to use these hidden resources.
Wanting desperately to achieve
taps that hidden resource
that every one of us has.

Herb Elliott
Distance Runner

Sometimes when I'm racing
and I'm really stroking strong,
I can feel the ice breaking away
beneath me.
It is a wonderful feeling
because it means
that I have reached the limit,
the ice can't hold me back anymore.
Confidence was the most important
quality for me to develop
before I could even think about
running the big races.

Eric Heiden
Speed Skater

CONFIDENCE

Webster's Collegiate Dictionary

Confidence: 1. full trust
2. belief in the powers
3. belief in oneself and one's powers or abilities
4. assurance

The Synonym Finder

Confidence: trust, faith, reliance, fortitude, security, sureness, positiveness, assurance, poise, coolness, calmness, spirit, spunk, heart, stamina, vigor, backbone, nerve, courage

Every time you go out on the ice, there are slight flaws. You can always think of something you should have done better.
These are the things you must work on.

Dorothy Hamill
Figure Skater

You never fail until you stop trying.

Florence Griffith Joyner
Sprinter

I always set so many goals for myself, but I did not come here saying I wanted a medal. I just wanted to dive well.

Mary Ellen Clark
Diver

On the ice I'm aggressive. To race is to go all out, every time, no matter what happens. I never worry about falling.

Bonnie Blair
Speed Skater

I was nervous,
so I read the New Testament.
I read the verse about no fear,
and I felt relaxed.
Then I jumped farther than
I ever jumped before in my life.

Willye White
Long Jumper

I'm convinced
that mental attitude
has a lot to do
with winning.

Ingemar Stenmark
Skier

I went out to win or die.

Ken McArthur
Marathoner

I enjoy doing things
that people don't think I can do.
I like proving them wrong.
I like the individual challenge.

Don Schollander
Swimmer

Every day in the car going back and forth to the skating rink to practice, I visualized the skating arena, the audience, my costume and my performance. I saw the standing ovation, heard the thunderous applause raising the roof.... I experienced every single emotion I had visualized.... It wasn't until the medal presentation when I was standing on the podium that I realized I wasn't dreaming. I knew because "The Star-Spangled Banner" was being played at a much faster tempo than it had been in my dream. It was then, and only then, that I knew this was the real thing. The dream had finally come true.

Brian Boitano
Figure Skater

I learned to win by learning to lose—
that means not being afraid of losing.
That probably helped me more than
any other single thing.

Jeff Blatnick
Greco-Roman Wrestler

I'm a schoolteacher back home, and I always tell the kids that whatever you're doing, always go 100 percent, full speed and give it your best. That's what I tried to do.

Damon Keeve
Judo

You don't ski by the book,
you ski by instinct.
The secret in the downhill is really
the ability to think ahead.

Toni Sailer
Skier

We all came together six months
before the 1980 Winter Olympics
with different styles of hockey and
different ethnic beliefs...but we made
ourselves a team. Individually, we
could not have done it.

Mike Eruzione
Hockey Player

You can't just work out.
You have to concentrate on what
you're doing in workouts.
There's a satisfaction when you have
a hard set, a rugged workout,
and you feel it, and you take it,
and go beyond it.

Tracy Caulkins
Swimmer

Naturally only one can steer.
But both have important jobs to fill.
A good start depends in large part
on the ability of the back man.
And also **teamwork** during the race
is a requirement for
that extra hundredth of a second.

Hans Rinn
Double Luge

TEAMWORK

Webster's Collegiate Dictionary

Teamwork: 1. cooperative or coordinated effort on the part of a group of persons
2. acting together
3. common cause
4. working together
5. subordinating personal prominence to the efficiency of the whole

The Synonym Finder

Teamwork: cooperation, collaboration, combined, joint action, interaction, pulling together, pooling, unison, coordination, harmony, synergy, concert, concurrent, concord

I want to win.
I'm here to win.

Ira Davis
Hop, Step and Jump

I just keep on running.
There is no secret about what makes
Zatopek tick.
It is just that.

Emil Zatopek
5,000 and 10,000 Meter

I just spent a little more time in the pool—
worked a little harder.

Janet Evans
Swimmer

One day I run 10 miles,
resting in the afternoon.
The next morning I do only
physical training and gymnastics.
The day after I run another 10-15 miles.
I play basketball, volleyball and tennis.
I play these sports about two hours,
then run some more.

Abebe Bikila
Marathoner

I just kept on a little faster.

El Ouafi
Marathoner

That one-tenth of a second
changed my life.

Buster Crabbe
Swimmer

The trouble is that
they do not want to train hard enough.

Fanny Blankers-Koen
200 Meter

George is nimble,
and George is quick.
Watch me, folks,
'cause I can really stick.

George Foreman
Boxer

I don't worry about winning or losing—
just getting to the end of the pool
as fast as I can.
Coming down the stretch,
I think about the same thing all the time.
Put your head down
and go as fast as you can—
put winning or losing out of your mind—
just concentrate on swimming
as fast as you can.

Janet Evans
Swimmer

In the closing seconds of every game,
I want the ball in my hands for that last
shot—not in anybody else's, not in
anybody else's hands in the world.

Larry Bird
Basketball Player

I just told myself that no matter
how much my ankle was killing me,
I wouldn't give in, I wouldn't limp.

Phil Mahre
Skier

I was jolly glad, though,
when I hit the tape.

Douglas Lowe
800 Meter

The medals aren't the important thing.
The glory is nice but it doesn't last.
It's all about performing well
and feeling deeply about it.

Daley Thompson
Decathlete

I've always believed
that the desire must come from within,
not as a result of being driven
by coaches or parents.

Dawn Fraser
Swimmer

It's competing
that matters.

Al Oerter
Discus Thrower

No coward
will ever
win.

Karl Schranz
Skier

WIN

Webster's Collegiate Dictionary

Win: 1. to finish first
2. to succeed by striving or effort
3. to gain the victory
4. to succeed in reaching
5. to overcome an adversary

The Synonym Finder

Win: finish first, come out ahead, sweep, triumph, conquer, prevail over, overcome, gain the prize, score a success, gain a victory, take by storm, reach, acquire, glean, accomplish

To win, I have to get angry.
My anger is directed at the course,
at attacking it and beating it.

Ingemar Stenmark
Skier

Inspiration is not enough to win such a
tough competition. Years of training
are necessary.

Ulrich Wehling
Skier

You learn pain in practice, and you will
know it in every race. As you approach the
limit of your endurance, it begins coming on
gradually, hitting your stomach first. Then
your arms grow heavy and your legs
tighten—thighs first, then the knees.
You sink lower in the water as though
someone was pushing down on your back.
You experience perception changes.
The sounds of the pool blend together and
become a crashing roar in your ears.
The water takes on a pinkish tinge.
Your stomach feels as though it's going to
fall out—every kick hurts like heck—and
suddenly you hear a shrill internal scream....
It is right here, at the pain barrier,
that the great competitors are separated
from the rest.

Don Schollander
Swimmer

The downhill does not leave room for a compromise. You're either in front or you perish.

Guy Perillat
Skier

Holding the mile record doesn't make it any easier to run a mile in the future.

Sebastian Coe
Distance Runner

If you are not afraid to go out and compete, then you will run your best race. But if you go out with a fear of something, even against yourself or against the clock, then you have lost the race before you start.

Jim Ryun
Distance Runner

I'll finish one, two, three, or break a leg.

Gaston Strobino
Marathoner

I knew if I stayed up with the leaders
and put on a good final kick I would win.
There were probably 75,000 screaming
people in the stadium, but all I could hear
was the throbbing of my heart.
I kept thinking, one more try, one more try.

Billy Mills
10,000 Meter

The difference between my methods and
others is great. The difference is that I
train more often and lift more weights than
others. I have become a great champion
because of my love of hard work and my
great striving to reach the target of victory.

Vasili Alexeyev
Weight Lifter

The secret to success is
doing the best that you can do.
Forget about whether you might win or
lose. By working hard and practicing the
skills that you need to perform,
the results will take care of themselves.
Being successful is doing your best.

Barbara Ann Cochran
Skier

All pressure is self-inflicted.
It's what you make of it—
or how you let it rub off on you.

Sebastian Coe
Distance Runner

Running is fun.
I enjoy competing.
That is all.

Lasse Viren
5,000 and 10,000 Meter

Before I was even into my teens,
I knew exactly what I wanted
to be when I grew up.
My goal was to be
the greatest athlete that ever lived.

Babe Didrikson
Runner

Some have wrestled
without great
skill;
none have wrestled
without **pride**.

Dan Gable
Wrestler

PRIDE

Webster's Collegiate Dictionary

Pride: 1. high opinion of one's dignity
2. the state or feeling of being proud
3. pleasure or satisfaction taken in something done by oneself
4. proper respect for oneself

The Synonym Finder

Pride: self respect, self-esteem, feelings, sensibilities, identity, proud, picture of oneself, glory in, self-image, pat oneself on the back

My strategy is simple.
I get out in front early—
run as hard as I can—
for as long as I can.

Steve Ovett
Distance Runner

Becoming number one is easier
than remaining number one.

Bill Bradley
Basketball Player

The payoff for all the preparation
is personal satisfaction,
seeing if I can be the best.

Greg Barton
Kayaker

I knew the only thing I could do
was shoot the match I've had
in my mind for so long.
I think it took a lot of struggling
over the years to finally put it together,
but now I know I can trust myself
with my goals and dreams.

Launi Meili
Shooter

That defeat
was the greatest thing
that ever happened to me
because all of a sudden
I knew
I could win.

Pat McCormick
Diver

But all I kept thinking was,
Run, kid, run.

Ray Barbuti
400 Meter

I didn't
want to quit
and say
for the rest
of my life,
"Well, maybe I
could have been..."

Frank Shorter
Distance Runner

100
Exciting Thoughts
Worthy of a
Gold Medal

To laugh is to **risk** appearing the fool.

To weep is to **risk** appearing sentimental.

To reach out for another is to **risk** involvement.

To expose feelings is to **risk** exposing your true self.

To place your ideas, your dreams, before a crowd is to **risk** their loss.

To love is to **risk** not being loved in return.

To live is to **risk** dying.

To hope is to **risk** despair.

To try is to **risk** failure.

But **risks** must be taken, because the greatest hazard in life is to **risk** nothing.

The person who **risks** nothing, does nothing, has nothing, and is nothing.

They may avoid suffering and sorrow, but they cannot learn, feel, change, grow, love, live.

Chained by their attitudes, they are a slave, they have forfeited their freedom.

Only a person who **risks** is free.

Author Unknown

RISK

Webster's Collegiate Dictionary

Risk: 1. exposure to the chance of loss
2. to venture upon
3. to take a chance
4. to expose to hazard

The Synonym Finder

Risk: danger, jeopardy, dare, venture,
gamble, tempt, try, attempt,
lay on the line, peril, leap,
unpredictability, exposure,
liability, uncertainty, speculation

If you think you are beaten, you are;
If you think that you dare not, you don't;
If you'd like to win, but you think you can't,
It's almost certain you won't.

If you think you'll lose, you've lost;
For out in the world you'll find
Success begins with a fellow's will.
It's all in the state of mind.

If you think you are outclassed, you are;
You've got to think high to rise;
You've got to be sure of yourself before
You can ever win a prize.

Life's battles don't always go
To the stronger or faster man;
But sooner or later the man who wins
Is the man who thinks he can.

Author Unknown

When a winner makes a mistake, he says,
"I was wrong;"
When a loser makes a mistake, he says,
"It wasn't my fault."

A winner works harder than a loser
and has more time;
A loser is always "too busy" to do
what is necessary.

A winner goes through a problem;
A loser goes around it, and never gets past it.

A winner makes commitments;
A loser makes promises.

A winner says,
"I'm good, but not as good as I ought to be;"
A loser says,
"I'm not as bad as a lot of other people."

A winner listens;
A loser just waits until it's his turn to talk.

A winner respects those who are superior to him
and tries to learn something from them;
A loser resents those who are superior to him
and tries to find chinks in their armor.

A winner feels responsible for more than his job;
A loser says, "I only work here."

A winner says, "There ought to be a
better way to do it;"
A loser says, "That's the way it's
always been done here."

Author Unknown

61

A crowd of troubles passed him by
As he with courage waited;
He said, "Where do you troubles fly
When you are thus belated?"
"We go," they say, "to those who mope,
Who look on life dejected,
Who meekly say 'good-bye' to hope,
We go where we're expected."

Francis J. Allison

The important thing is
not to stop questioning.
Curiosity has its own reason for existing.
One cannot help but be in awe when
he contemplates the mysteries of eternity,
of life, of the marvelous structure of reality.
It is enough if one tries merely
to comprehend a little
of this mystery every day.
Never lose a holy curiosity.

Albert Einstein

No one ever attains
very eminent success
by simply doing what is
required of him; it is
the amount and excellence
of what is over and above
the required that
determines the greatness
of ultimate distinction.

Charles Kendall Adams

To put the world right in order, we must
first put the nation in order;
to put the nation in order, we must first
put the family in order;
to put the family in order, we must first
cultivate our personal life;
we must first set our hearts right.

Confucius

First, Plant Five Rows of P's.
Presence, Promptness, Preparation,
Perseverance, **Patience.**

Next, Plant Three Rows of Squash.
Squash gossip, Squash indifference,
Squash unjust criticism.

Then Plant Five Rows of Lettuce.
Let us be faithful to duty,
Let us be unselfish and loyal,
Let us obey the rules and regulations,
Let us be true to our obligations,
Let us love one another.

No Garden is Complete Without Turnips.
Turn up for meetings, Turn up with a smile,
Turn up with new ideas, Turn up with
determination to make everything
count for something good and worthwhile.

Author Unknown

PATIENT

Webster's Collegiate Dictionary

Patient: 1. bearing pains or trials calmly or without complaint
2. manifesting forbearance under provocation or strain
3. steadfast despite opposition, difficulty or adversity
4. working steadily without giving up

The Synonym Finder

Patient: calm, quiet, serene, unruffled, unflappable, placid, peaceful, poised, balanced, steady, self-controlled, collected, relaxed, persistent, unremitting, uncompromising, firm

If you can't do great things,
do small things in a great way.
Don't wait for great opportunities.
Seize common, everyday ones
and make them great.

Napoleon Hill

Wise men say, and not without reason,
that whoever wished to foresee the future
might consult the past.

Machiavelli

You are the man who used to boast
That you'd achieve the uttermost,
some day.

You merely wished a show, to demonstrate
How much you know
And prove the distance you can go...

Another year we've just passed through,
What new ideas came to you? How many
Big things did you do?

Time...left twelve fresh months in your care.
How many of them did you share
With opportunity and dare again
Where you so often missed?

We do not find you on the list
of MAKERS GOOD.
Explain the fact!
Ah no, 'Twas not the chance you lacked,
As usual—you failed to ACT!!!

Author Unknown

One ship drives east,
and another west
With the self-same winds that blow;
'Tis the set of the sails
And not the gales,
Which decides the way we go.

Like the winds of the sea
are the ways of fate,
As they voyage along through life;
'Tis the will of the soul
That decides its goal,
And not the calm or the strife.

Ella Wheeler Wilcox

For every ailment under the sun,
There is a remedy, or there is none;
If there be one, try to find it;
If there be none, never mind it.

Mother Goose Rhyme

Do more than exist, live.
Do more than touch, feel.
Do more than look, observe.
Do more than read, absorb.
Do more than hear, listen.
Do more than listen, understand.
Do more than think, ponder.
Do more than talk, say something.

John H. Rhoades

Love work.
Turn a deaf ear to slander.
Be considerate in correcting others.
Do not be taken up by trifles.
Do not resent plain speaking.
Meet offenders half-way.
Be thorough in thought.
Have an open mind.
Do your duty without grumbling.

Marcus Aurelius

There are four steps to accomplishment:
Plan purposefully.
Prepare prayerfully.
Proceed positively.
Pursue **persistently**.

Author Unknown

PERSIST

Webster's Collegiate Dictionary

Persist:
1. to continue steadfastly or firmly in some state, purpose or course of action in spite of opposition
2. to last
3. to endure tenaciously
4. to refuse to give up
5. to last for some time

The Synonym Finder

Persist: remain, last, keep on, subsist, survive, carry on, stay, stand firm, hang in there, be permanent, remain valid, steadfast, grind, sustain, maintain, uphold

ANOTHER TACK

When you suspect you're going wrong,
Or lack the strength to move along
With placid poise among your peers,
Because of haunting doubts or fears:
It's time for you to shift your pack,
And steer upon another tack!

When wind and waves assail your ship,
And anchors from the bottom slip;
When clouds of mist obscure your sun,
And foaming waters madly run:
It's time for you to change your plan,
And make a port while yet you can!

When men laugh at your woeful plight,
And seek your old repute to blight;
When all the world bestows a frown,
While you are sliding swiftly down:
It's time for you to show your grit,
And let the scoffers know you're fit!

When Failure opens your luckless door,
And struts across the creaking floor;
When Fortune flees and leaves you bare,
And former friends but coldly stare:
It's time for you to take a tack,
And show the world you're "coming back!"

Lilburn Harwood Townsend

Your greatness is measured
by your kindness—
Your education and intellect
by your modesty—
Your ignorance is betrayed
by your suspicions and prejudices—
Your real caliber is measured
by the consideration and tolerance
you have for others.

Wm. J. H. Boetcker

Not for one single day
Can I discern my way,
But this I surely know—

Who gives the day
Will show the way,
So I securely go.

John Oxenham

THE 10 COMMANDMENTS FOR SUCCESS

1. Persistence
2. **Challenge**
3. Imagination
4. Desire
5. Belief in truth and self
6. Determination
7. Enthusiasm
8. Practice
9. Development
10. Positive self-talk

THE 10 COMMANDMENTS FOR FAILURE

1. Worry
2. Doubt
3. Self-pity
4. Can't do it
5. Put it off
6. Complain
7. Hate
8. Quitter
9. Indecision
10. Run self down

Author Unknown

CHALLENGE

Webster's Collegiate Dictionary

Challenge: 1. to stimulate
2. something that by its nature or character serves as a call to a special effort
3. to dare
4. to call for skill, effort or imagination

The Synonym Finder

Challenge: call, summon, dare, affront, attack, question, charge, venture, risk, brave, face, stand up to, disagree, oppose, invite, arouse, stimulate, inspire, excite

If you simply take up the matter
of defending a mistake,
there will be no hope of improvement.

Winston Churchill

Life is a gift to be used every day,
Not to be smothered and hidden away;
It isn't a thing to be stored in the chest
Where you gather your keepsakes
and treasure your best;
It isn't a joy to be sipped now and then
And promptly put back
in a dark place again.

Life is a gift that the humblest may boast of
And one that the humblest
may well make the most of.
Get out and live it each hour of the day,
Wear it and use it as much as you may;
Don't keep it in niches and corners
and grooves,
You'll find that in service
its beauty improves.

Edgar A. Guest

SEVEN NATIONAL CRIMES

I don't think.
I don't know.
I don't care.
I am too busy.
I "leave well enough alone."
I have no time to read and find out.
I am not interested.

William J. H. Boetcker

God grant me the serenity
To accept the things I cannot change,
The courage to change the things I can,
And the wisdom to know the difference.

Reinhold Niebuhr

If you can dream and not
make dreams your master;
If you can think and not
make thoughts your aim;
If you can meet with triumph
and disaster;
And treat those two impostors
just the same,

If you can force your heart,
and nerve, and sinew
To serve your turn long after
they are gone;
And so hold on when
there is nothing in you
Except the will which says to them,
"Hold on,"

If you can fill the unforgiving minute
With sixty seconds' worth of distance run,
Yours is the earth
and everything that's in it,
And, what is more, you'll be a man, my son.

Rudyard Kipling

Success is to be measured
not so much by the position
that one has reached in life
as by the obstacles
which he has overcome
while trying to succeed.

Booker T. Washington

A NATION'S STRENGTH

What makes a nation's pillars high
And its foundations strong?
What makes it mighty to defy
The foes that round it throng?

It is not gold. Its kingdoms grand
Go down in battle shock;
Its shafts are laid on sinking sand,
Not on abiding rock.

Is it the sword? Ask the red dust
Of empires passed away;
The blood has turned their stones to rust,
Their glory to decay.

And is it pride? Ah, that bright crown
Has seemed to nations sweet;
But God has struck its luster down
In ashes at his feet.

Not gold but only men can make
A people great and strong;
Men who for truth and honor's sake
Stand fast and suffer long.

Brave men who work while others sleep,
Who dare while others fly—
They build a nation's pillars deep
And lift them to the sky.

Ralph Waldo Emerson

FOUNDATION STONES

In building a firm foundation for success, here are a few stones to remember:

1. The wisdom of preparation.
2. The value of confidence.
3. The worth of honesty.
4. The privilege of working.
5. The discipline of struggle.
6. The magnetism of character.
7. The radiance of health.
8. The forcefulness of simplicity.
9. The winsomeness of courtesy.
10. The attractiveness of modesty.
11. The inspiration of cleanliness.
12. The satisfaction of serving.
13. The power of suggestion.
14. The buoyancy of **enthusiasm**.
15. The advantage of initiative.
16. The virtue of patience.
17. The rewards of cooperation.
18. The fruitfulness of perseverance.
19. The sportsmanship of losing.
20. The joy of winning.

Rollo C. Hester

ENTHUSIASM

Webster's Collegiate Dictionary

Enthusiasm:
1. lively interest
2. absorbing or controlling possession of the mind by any pursuit
3. ardent zeal
4. a strong liking

The Synonym Finder

Enthusiasm: eagerness, earnestness, keenness, intensity, excitement, fervor, warmth, glow, fire, devotion, zeal, passion, spirit, liveliness, vitality, life, bounce, determination

Take time to laugh
It is the music of the soul.
Take time to think
It is the source of power.
Take time to play
It is the source of perpetual youth.
Take time to read
It is the fountain of wisdom.
Take time to pray
It is the greatest power on earth.
Take time to love and be loved
It is a God-given privilege.
Take time to be friendly
It is the road to happiness.
Take time to give
It is too short a day to be selfish.
Take time to work
It is the price of success.

Author Unknown

Life is currently described as
one of four ways:
as a journey, as a battle,
as a pilgrimage, and as a race.
Select your own metaphor,
but the finishing necessity is all the same.
For if life is a journey,
it must be completed.
If life is a battle, it must be finished.
If life is a pilgrimage, it must be concluded.
And if life is a race, it must be won.

J. Richard Sneed

When things go wrong,
as they sometimes will,
When the road you're trudging
seems all uphill,
When the funds are low
and the debts are high,
And you want to smile,
but you have to sigh,
When care is pressing you down a bit—
Rest if you must, but don't you quit.

Life is queer with its twists and turns,
As every one of us sometimes learns,
And many a person turns about
When they might have won
had they stuck it out.
Don't give up though
the pace seems slow—
You may succeed with another blow.

Often the struggler has given up
When he might have captured
the victor's cup;
And he learned too late when
the night came down,
How close he was to the golden crown.

Success is failure turned inside out,
So stick to the fight
when you're hardest hit—
It's when things seem worst
that you mustn't quit.

Author Unknown

FAILURES

'Tis better to have tried in vain,
Sincerely striving for a goal,
Than to have lived upon the plain
An idle and a timid soul.

'Tis better to have fought and spent
Your **courage**, missing all applause,
Than to have lived in smug content
And never ventured for a cause.

For he who tries and fails may be
The founder of the better day;
Though never his the victory,
From him shall others learn the way.

Edgar A. Guest

COURAGE

Webster's Collegiate Dictionary

Courage:
1. the quality of mind or spirit that enables a person to face difficulty without fear
2. bravery
3. the heart as a source of emotion
4. the quality of being able to control one's fear

The Synonym Finder

Courage: fortitude, endurance, tenacity, heart, will power, firmness, pluck, invincibleness, steadfastness, spirit, backbone, nerve, grit, moxie, spunk, determination

WHY WORRY?

There are only two things to worry about;
Either you are well or you are sick.

If you are well, then there is nothing
to worry about;
But if you are sick, there are two things
to worry about;
Either you will get well, or you will die.

If you get well, there is nothing
to worry about.
If you die, there are only two things
to worry about;
Either you will go to Heaven or Hell.

If you go to Heaven, there is nothing
to worry about.
But if you go to Hell,
you'll be so darn busy
shaking hands with people you know,
You won't have time to worry.

Author Unknown

It's not just looking at the present.
It's seeing into the future.

It's not just having goals.
It's having strategies to achieve them
and the courage to pursue them.

It's being so convinced you're right
that other people
believe you're right, too.

It's feeling that failure is simply
unacceptable.

Author Unknown

For all your days prepare,
And meet them ever alike:
When you are the anvil, bear—
When you are the hammer, strike.

Edwin Markham

Happy the man, and happy he alone,
He, who can call today his own;
He who, secure within, can say:
"Tomorrow, do thy worst,
for I have liv'd today."

Horace

The moral of this story
Is very plain to see,
Take yourself to task today,
Tomorrow you'll be free.

Do it now; it's not so hard,
And when it's done, it's done.
The next day pays the dividends,
And provides some time for fun.

Success is not tomorrow;
Success is in today.
Do it now! Get it done!
Success is on the way.

Author Unknown

If you can't be a pine on the top of the hill,
Be a scrub in the valley—but be
The **best** little scrub by the side of the hill;
Be a bush, if you can't be a tree.

If you can't be a bush, be a bit of the grass,
And some highway happier make;
If you can't be a muskie, then just be a bass—
But the liveliest bass in the lake.

We can't all be captains, we've got to be crew,
There's something for all of us here.
There's big work to do and there's lesser to do
And the task we must do is the near.

If you can't be a highway, then just be a trail,
If you can't be the sun, be a star;
It isn't by size that you win or you fail—
Be the **best** of whatever you are.

Douglas Malloch

BEST

Webster's Collegiate Dictionary

Best:
1. the highest quality
2. most advantageous
3. with much success or in the highest degree
4. being the most
5. the most that can be done

The Synonym Finder

Best: excellent, unsurpassed, super, select, first-class, top, peak, prime, zenith, apex, utmost, finest, foremost, greatly, right, correct, fitting, outstanding, highest

RULES FOR BUSINESS SUCCESS

Carefully examine every detail
of the business.
Be prompt.
Take time to consider and then
decide quickly.
Dare to go forward.
Bear your trouble patiently.
Maintain your integrity as a sacred thing.
Never tell business lies.
Make no useless acquaintances.
Never try to appear something
more than you are.
Pay your debts promptly.
Learn how to risk your money
at the right time.
Employ your time well.
Do not reckon on chance.
Be polite to everyone.
Never be discouraged.
Work hard and you will succeed.

Rothschild

Look to this day!
For it is life, the very life of life.
In its brief course
Lie all the verities and realities
of your existence:
The bliss of growth
The glory of action
The splendor of beauty,
For yesterday is but a dream
And tomorrow is only a vision,
But today well lived makes every yesterday
a dream of happiness
And every tomorrow a vision of hope.
Look well, therefore, to this day!
Such is the salutation to the dawn.

Kalidasa

It is not the critic who counts;
not the man who points out
how the strong man stumbled,
or where the doer of deeds
could have done better.
The credit belongs to the man
who is actually in the arena;
whose face is marred by dust
and sweat and blood;
who strives valiantly;
who errs and comes short
again and again;
who knows the great enthusiasms,
the great devotions,
and spends himself in a worthy cause;
who at the best knows in the end
the triumph of high achievement;
and who at the worst, if he fails,
at least fails while daring greatly;
so that his place shall never be
with those cold and timid souls
who know neither victory nor defeat.

Theodore Roosevelt

A man's life is interesting
primarily when he has failed—I well know.
For it's a sign that he had
tried to surpass himself.

Georges Clemenceau

Unless each day can be
looked back upon by an individual
as one in which he has had some fun,
some joy, some real satisfaction,
that day is a loss.
It is un-Christian and wicked,
in my opinion,
to allow such a thing to occur.

Dwight D. Eisenhower

PERSISTENCE

Nothing in the world
can take the place of persistence.
Talent will not;
nothing is more common than
unsuccessful men with talent.
Genius will not;
unrewarded genius is almost a proverb.
Education will not;
the world is full of educated derelicts.
Persistence and determination
alone are omnipotent.
The slogan "Press On" has solved
and always will solve
the problems of the human race.

Calvin Coolidge

"What is the real good?"
I ask in musing mood.

"Order," said the law court;
"Knowledge," said the school;
"Truth," said the wise man;
"Pleasure," said the fool;
"Love," said the maiden;
"Beauty," said the page;
"Freedom," said the dreamer;
"Home," said the sage;
"Fame," said the soldier;
"Equity," said the seer.
Spake my heart fully sad:
"The answer is not here."

Then within my bosom
Softly this I heard:
"Each heart holds the secret:
'Kindness' is the word."

John Boyle O'Reilly

May every soul that touches mine—
Be it the slightest contact—
Get therefrom some good;
Some little grace; one kindly thought;
One aspiration yet unfelt;
One bit of courage
For the darkening sky;
One gleam of faith
To brave the thickening ills of **life**;
One glimpse of brighter skies
Beyond the gathering mists—
To make this **life** worthwhile.

George Eliot

LIFE

Webster's Collegiate Dictionary

Life: 1. the force that makes or keeps something alive
2. a person that enlivens
3. a living thing
4. liveliness or energy
5. a vital being

The Synonym Finder

Life: existence, generation, human, liveliness, spirit, zest, flair, zing, warmth, glow, dazzle, brilliance, cheer, sparkle, vigor, energy, passion, enthusiasm, zeal, soul, elasticity, bounce

Do all the good you can,
By all the means you can,
In all the ways you can,
In all the places you can,
At all the times you can,
To all the people you can,
As long as ever you can.

John Wesley

To dream anything that you want to dream; that is the beauty of the human mind. To do anything that you want to do; that is the strength of the human will. To trust yourself to test your limits; that is the courage to succeed.

Bernard Edmonds

To look up and not down,
To look forward and not back,
To look out and not in, and
To lend a hand.

Edward Everett Hale

Slow me down, Lord!
Ease the pounding of my heart
by the quieting of my mind.
Steady my hurried pace,
With a vision of the eternal reach of time.
Give me, amidst the confusion of my day,
The calmness of the everlasting hills.
Break the tension of my nerves
With the soothing music
of the singing streams
That live in my memory.
Help me to know the magical
restoring power of sleep.
Teach me the art of taking
minute vacations of slowing down.
To look at a flower;
To chat with an old friend
or make a new one;
To pat a stray dog;
To watch a spider build a web;
To smile at a child;
Or to read from a good book.
Remind me each day
That the race is not always to the swift;
That there is more to life
than increasing its speed.
Let me look upward into the towering oak
And know that it grew great and strong
Because it grew slowly and well.

Orin L. Crain

We are all
faced with a
series of **opportunities**,
beautifully
disguised as
unsolvable problems.

Author Unknown

OPPORTUNITY

Webster's Collegiate Dictionary

Opportunity: 1.   an appropriate or favor-
             able time or occasion
        2.   a situation or condition
             favorable for attainment
             of a goal
        3.   a good position or
             prospect
        4.   a good chance

The Synonym Finder

Opportunity: favorable time, good
             moment, perfect occasion,
             right set of circumstances,
             possibility, opening,
             chance, appropriate,
             correct, fortune, good

With every rising of the sun,
Think of your life as just begun.
The past has shrived and buried deep
All yesterdays; there let them sleep.

Concern yourself with but today,
Woo it, and teach it to obey
Your will and wish. Since time began
Today has been the friend of man.

Ella Wheeler Wilcox

I have been given this day to use as I will.
I can waste it or use it for good.
What I choose to do is important,
because I am exchanging
a day of my life for it.

Author Unknown

A man can be as great as he wants to be,
if a man believes in himself,
if he has the determination,
the courage,
the dedication
and the competitive drive,
if you are willing to sacrifice the little things
in life and pay the price for the
things that are worthwhile,
it can be done.
Once a man has made a commitment
to a way of life,
he puts the greatest strength in the work
behind him,
something we call heart power,
once a man has made this commitment,
nothing will stop him
short of success.

Vince Lombardi

What is Life?

Life is a gift...accept it
Life is an adventure...dare it
Life is a mystery...unfold it
Life is a game...play it
Life is a struggle...face it
Life is beauty...praise it
Life is a puzzle...solve it
Life is opportunity...take it
Life is sorrowful...experience it
Life is a song...sing it
Life is a goal...achieve it
Life is a mission...fulfill it.

Author Unknown

There is a destiny that makes us brothers:
None goes his way alone;
All that we send into the lives of others
Comes back into our own.

Edwin Markham

Never put off till to-morrow
what you can do to-day.
Never trouble another for
what you can do yourself.
Never spend your money
before you have earned it.
Never buy what you do not
want because it is cheap.
Pride costs more than hunger,
thirst and cold.
We seldom report of having
eaten too little.
Nothing is troublesome that we do willingly.
How much pain evils have cost us that
have never happened!
Take things always by the smooth handle.
When angry, count ten before you speak,
if very angry, count a hundred.

Thomas Jefferson

TWELVE THINGS TO REMEMBER

The value of time.

The success of perseverance.

The pleasure of **working**.

The dignity of simplicity.

The worth of character.

The power of kindness.

The influence of example.

The obligation of duty.

The wisdom of economy.

The virtue of patience.

The improvement of talent.

The joy of origination.

Marshall Field

WORK

Webster's Collegiate Dictionary

Work: 1. exertion or effort directed to produce or accomplish something
2. productive activity
3. the result of labor
4. the use of energy or skill
5. something to be done

The Synonym Finder

Work: exertion, effort, endeavor, sweat, discipline, undertaking, duty, mission, service, call, deed, performance, action, feat, accomplishment, creation, movement, result, play, drive, attain

QUALITY OF LIFE

Realize that each human being has a built-in capacity for recuperation and repair.

Recognize that the quality of life
is all-important.

Assume responsibility for the quality
of your own life.

Nurture the regenerative and restorative
forces within you.

Utilize laughter to create a mood in which
the other positive emotions can be put to
work for yourself and those around you.

Develop confidence and the ability
to feel love, hope and faith,
and acquire a strong will to live.

Norman Cousins

When a thing is done, it's done.
Don't look back.
Look forward to your next objective.

General George C. Marshall

A CREED

To be so strong that nothing can disturb your peace of mind; to talk health, happiness and prosperity; to make your friends feel that there is something in them; to look on the sunny side of everything; to think only of the best; to be just as enthusiastic about the success of others as you are about your own; to forget the mistakes of the past and profit by them; to wear a cheerful countenance and give a smile to everyone you meet; to be too large for worry, too noble for anger, too strong for fear, and too happy to permit the presence of trouble.

Christian D. Larson

One ought never to turn one's back on a threatened danger and try to run away from it. If you do that, you will double the danger. But if you meet it promptly and without flinching, you will reduce the danger by half. Never run away from anything. Never!

Winston Churchill

THE DECLARATION OF INDEPENDENCE

When, in the course of human events, it becomes necessary for one people to dissolve the political bands which have connected them with another, and to assume, among the powers of the earth, the separate and equal station to which the laws of nature and of nature's God entitle them, a decent respect to the opinions of mankind requires that they should declare the causes which impel them to the separation.

We hold these truths to be self-evident: that all men are created equal; that they are endowed by their Creator with certain inalienable rights; that among these are life, liberty, and the pursuit of **happiness**.

HAPPY

Webster's Collegiate Dictionary

Happy: 1. delighted, pleased or glad
2. favored by fortune
3. contented
4. great pleasure

The Synonym Finder

Happy: delighted, glad, pleased,
content, gratified, satisfied,
well-pleased, thrilled, tickled,
cheerful, high spirits,
optimistic, positive, upbeat,
untroubled, laughing, timely,
expedient

I am only one, but I *am* one.
I can't do everything,
but I *can* do something.
And what I *can* do, that I ought to do.
And what I *ought* to do, by the grace of God,
I *shall* do.

Edward Hale

RULE #1

Don't sweat the small stuff.

RULE #2

It's all small stuff.

Author Unknown

Suppose everybody cared enough,
everybody shared enough,
wouldn't everybody have enough?
There is enough in the world
for everyone's need,
but not enough for everyone's greed.

Frank Buchman

Class never runs scared. It is sure-footed and confident in the knowledge that you can meet life head on and handle whatever comes along.

Class never makes excuses. It takes its lumps and learns from past mistakes.

Class is considerate of others. It knows that good manners is nothing more than a series of petty sacrifices. Class bespeaks an aristocracy that has nothing to do with ancestors or money. The most affluent blue-blood can be totally without class while the descendant of a Welsh miner may ooze class from every pore.

Class never tries to build itself up by tearing others down. Class is already up and need not strive to look better by making others look worse.

Class can "walk with kings and keep its virtue and talk with crowds and keep the common touch." Everyone is comfortable with the person who has class—because he is comfortable with himself.

If you have class you don't need much of anything else. If you don't have it, no matter what else you have—it doesn't make much difference.

Author Unknown

Thoughts are the pinions of the soul,
And carry far when they're set free,
And if they're good, great good they'll do
And benefit both you and me;
So we should gladly do our share
Of worthwhile work and thinking, too;
And spread the thoughts of brotherhood—
Think thoughts that none have cause to rue.

Alonzo Newton Benn

Time is
Too slow for those who Wait,
Too swift for those who Fear,
Too long for those who Grieve;
Too short for those who Rejoice;
But for those who Love,
Time is Eternity.

Henry Van Dyke

Just for today I will be happy. This assumes what Abraham Lincoln said is true, that "most folks are about as happy as they make up their minds to be." Happiness is from within; it is not a matter of externals.

Just for today I will take care of my body. I will exercise it, care for it, nourish it, not abuse it nor neglect it, so that it will be a perfect machine for my bidding.

Just for today I will try to strengthen my mind. I will learn something useful. I will not be a mental loafer. I will read something that requires effort, thought and concentration.

Just for today I will exercise my soul in three ways. I will do somebody a good turn and not get found out. I will do at least two things I don't want to do, as William James suggests, just for exercise.

Just for today I will be agreeable. I will look as well as I can, dress as becomingly as possible, talk low, act courteously, be liberal with praise, criticize not at all, nor find fault with anything and not try to regulate nor improve anyone.

Just for today I will try to live through this day only, not to tackle my whole life problem at once. I can do things for twelve hours that would appall me if I had to keep them up for a lifetime.

Just for today I will have a program. I will write down what I expect to do every hour. I may not follow it exactly, but I will have it. I will eliminate two pests, hurry and indecision.

Sybyl F. Partridge

Learn to get along with people.
Learn to exhibit more patience
than any other man you know.
Learn to respect other men's
ideas and opinions.
Learn to think problems through
to the end.
Learn to try to put yourself in the
other fellow's place.
Be democratic.
Be loyal.
Cultivate cheerfulness.
WORK.

Harry J. Klingler

LEARN

Webster's Collegiate Dictionary

Learn: 1. to acquire knowledge of or
              skill in by study
              2. to become informed of or
              acquainted with
              3. to gain by experience
              4. to fix in the mind

The Synonym Finder

Learn: comprehend, realize, ascertain,
              determine, discover, glean,
              acquire, receive, absorb, digest,
              assimilate, take in, understand,
              apprehend

CAST OF CHARACTERS

I Won't is a tramp,
I Can't is a quitter,
I Don't Know is lazy,
I Wish I Could is a wisher,
I Might is waking up,
I Will Try is on his feet,
I Can is on his way,
I Will is at work,
I Did is now the boss.

Earl Cassel

Three men were laying brick.
The first was asked, "What are you doing?"
He answered, "Laying some brick."
The second man was asked,
"What are you working for?"
He answered, "Five dollars a day."
The third man was asked,
"What are you doing?"
He answered,
"I'm helping to build a great cathedral."
Which man are you?

Charles Schwab

There is so much good
in the worst of us and
so much bad in the best of us
that it ill becomes
any of us
to find fault
with the rest of us.

Author Unknown

Lord yesterday I asked for
all things that I may enjoy life.
Today you gave me life that
I may enjoy all things.

Author Unknown

Be yourself—but be your best self.
Dare to be different
and to follow your own star.
And don't be afraid to be happy.
Believe that those you love, love you.

Author Unknown

May the road rise to meet you.
May the wind be always at your back.
May the sun shine warm on your face,
the rains fall soft upon your fields and, until
we meet again, may God hold you
in the palm of his hand.

An Irish Prayer

I shall pass through this world but once.
If therefore, there be any kindness
I can show,
or any good thing I can do,
let me do it now...for
I shall not pass this way again.

Etienne De Grellet

Have you actually measured up?
If you don't have that courage
to look at yourself and say,
Well, I failed miserably there,
I hurt someone's feelings needlessly,
I lost my temper—which you must never do
except deliberately—
you don't measure up
to your own standards.

Dwight D. Eisenhower

Four things a man must learn to do
If he would make his record true;
To think without confusion clearly;
To love his fellow-men sincerely;
To act from honest motives purely;
To trust in God and Heaven securely.

Henry Van Dyke

You know what you don't like to do,
But do you know what you do like to do?

Author Unknown

A great deal of **TALENT** is lost in the world for want of a little courage. Every day sends to their graves obscure men whom timidity prevented from making a first effort; who, if they could have been induced to begin, would in all probability have gone to great lengths in the career of fame. The fact is that to do anything in the world worth doing, we must not stand back shivering and thinking of the cold and danger, but jump in and scramble through as well as we can. It will not do to be perpetually calculating risks and adjusting nice changes; it did very well before the Flood, when a man would consult his friends upon an intended publication for a hundred and fifty years, and live to see his success afterward; but at present, a man waits, and doubts, and consults his brother, and his particular friends, till one day he finds he is sixty years old and that he has lost so much time in consulting cousins and friends that he has no more time to follow their advice.

Sydney Smith

TALENT

Webster's Collegiate Dictionary

Talent:
1. a special ability
2. capacity for achievement
3. a power of mind
4. developed by study and practice

The Synonym Finder

Talent: gift, endowment, genius, flair, knack, aptitude, ingenuity, cleverness, capacity, potentiality, power, skill, efficiency, know-how, mastery

I play it cool and dig all jive.
That's the reason I stay alive.
My motto, as I live and learn,
is dig and be dug in return.

Langston Hughes

Do you wish to roam farther and farther?
See! The Good lies so near.
Only learn to seize good fortune,
For good fortune's always here.

Johann Wolfgang von Goethe

Never worry about anything that is past.
Charge it up to experience and
forget the trouble.
There are always plenty of troubles ahead,
so don't turn and look back
on any behind you.

Herbert Hoover

It is easy enough to be happy,
When life flows by like a song,
But the man worth while,
Is the man with a smile,
When everything goes dead wrong.

Author Unknown

"It can't be done,"
never yet accomplished anything.
"I will try,"
has performed wonders.

Author Unknown

Would you like to have more courage? Here are five short rules, which, if you will follow them, I guarantee will increase your store of fortitude.

1. Act as if you were courageous. This makes you a bit braver, as if one side of yourself had been challenged and wished to show it was not wholly afraid.

2. Pause to reflect that others have had to face great discouragements and great obstacles and have overcome them. And what others have done, surely you can do.

3. Remember that your life forces move in a sort of rhythm and that if you feel depressed and without the power to face life you may be at the bottom of the trough; if you will keep up your courage, you will probably swing out of it by the very forces which at the moment are sucking you down.

4. Remember you feel more defeated and downcast at night than during the daylight hours. Courage comes with the sun.

5. Courage is the measure of a big soul. Try to measure up.

Dale Carnegie

To remain whole, be twisted!
To become straight, let yourself be bent.
To become full, be hollow.
Be tattered, that you may be renewed.

Lao Tzu

Sitting still and wishing
Makes no person great.
The good Lord sends the fishing
But you have to dig the bait.

Author Unknown

One of the commonest mistakes
and one of the costliest is thinking that
success is due to some genius,
some magic—something or other
which we do not possess.
Success is generally due to holding on,
and failure to letting go.
You decide to learn a language,
study music, take a course of reading,
train yourself physically.
Will it be **success** or failure?
It depends upon how much pluck and
perseverance that word "decide" contains.
The decision that nothing can overrule,
the grip that nothing can detach
will bring **success**.
Remember the Chinese proverb,
"With time and patience,
the mulberry leaf becomes satin."

Maltbie D. Babcock

SUCCESS

Webster's Collegiate Dictionary

Success: 1. the favorable or prosperous termination of attempts or endeavors
2. the attainment of honors
3. a successful performance or achievement
4. a satisfactory outcome

The Synonym Finder

Success: attainment, accomplishment, winner, triumph, victory, stroke of genius, good fortune, prosperity, good life, prosper, thrive, boom, gain, hit, achievement

The time of day I do not tell,
As some do, by the clock,
Or by the distant chiming bells
Set on some steeple rack,
But by the progress that I see
In what I have to do.
It's either Done O'clock to me,
Or only Half-Past Through.

John Kendrick Bangs

One of the illusions of life is that
the present hour is not the critical, decisive
hour. Write it on your heart that
every day is the best day of the year.

Ralph Waldo Emerson

When the world trembles, I'm unmoved;
When cloudy, I'm serene;
When darkness covers all without,
I'm always bright within.

Daniel Defoe

What is the recipe for successful achievement? To my mind there are just four essential ingredients: Choose a career you love.... Give it the best there is in you.... Seize your opportunities.... And be a member of the team. In no country but America, I believe, is it possible to fulfill all four of these requirements.

Benjamin F. Fairless

You're sick of the game!
"Well, now, that's a shame."

You're young and you're brave
and you're bright.
"You've had a raw deal!"
I know—but don't squeal.
Buck up, do your damnedest, and fight.
It's the plugging away
that will win you the day,
So don't be a piker, old pard!
Just draw on your grit; it's so easy to quit:
It's the keeping-your-chin-up that's hard.

It's easy to cry that you're beaten—and die.
It's easy to crawfish and crawl;
But to fight and to fight
when hope's out of sight,
Why, that's the best game of them all!
And though you come out
of each grueling bout
All broken and beaten and scarred,
Just have one more try—
it's dead easy to die,
It's the keeping-on-living that's hard.

Robert W. Service

Opportunity has a sly habit of slipping in the back door, and often comes disguised as misfortune, or temporary defeat.
Perhaps this is why so many people fail to recognize opportunity.

Napoleon Hill

'Twixt the optimist and pessimist
The difference is droll:
The optimist sees the doughnut
But the pessimist sees the hole.

McLandburgh Wilson

The spirit,

that is the will to win,

and the will to **excel**

are the things that endure.

These qualities

are so much more important

than events that occur.

Vince Lombardi

EXCEL

Webster's Collegiate Dictionary

Excel: 1. to surpass in accomplishment
2. to be distinguishable
3. to be greater or better

The Synonym Finder

Excel: surpass, exceed, eclipse, outdo, distance, top, outplay, advantage, dominate, tower above, stand out, outshine, beat, outdistance, come out on top

Every spirit makes its house;
but afterwards the house
confines the spirit.

Ralph Waldo Emerson

100
Powerful Phrases
with a
Silver Lining

Yesterday is a cancelled check;
tomorrow is a promissory note;
today is the only cash you have—
so spend it wisely.

Kay Lyons

It is never safe to look into the future
with eyes of fear.

Edward Henry Harriman

Do not wish to be anything
but what you are,
and try to be that perfectly.

St. Francis De Sales

You can't build a reputation on
what you're going to do.

Henry Ford

Well done is better than well said.

Ben Franklin

Why should we be in such
desperate haste to succeed,
and in such desperate enterprises?
If a man does not keep pace
with his companions,
perhaps it is because
he hears a different drummer.

Henry David Thoreau

Procrastination—
the art of keeping up
with yesterday.

Don Marquis

Don't belittle—be big.

Author Unknown

Hold yourself **responsible**
for a higher standard
than anybody
else expects of you.

Henry Ward Beecher

RESPONSIBLE

Webster's Collegiate Dictionary

Responsible: 1. answerable or accountable
                   2. chargeable for what occurs
                   3. having the capacity for
                       moral decisions
                   4. reliable
                   5. to take care of

The Synonym Finder

Responsible: answerable, accountable, liable, obligated, duty-bound, dependable, conscientious, hardworking, moral, ethical, upright, trustworthy, creditable, honest, faithful

The rung of a ladder was never meant
to rest upon, but only to hold a man's foot
long enough to enable him
to put the other somewhat higher.

Thomas Huxley

Unless you try to do something
beyond what you have already mastered,
you will never grow.

Ronald E. Osborn

Failure is only the opportunity to begin
again more intelligently.

Henry Ford

One of the saddest experiences which can come to a human being is to awaken, gray-haired and wrinkled, near the close of an unproductive career, to the fact that all through the years he has been using only a small part of himself.

V.W. Burrows

Take a chance!
All life is a chance.
The man who goes furthest is generally
the one who is willing to do and dare.
The "sure thing" boat
never gets far from shore.

Dale Carnegie

Success is a journey, not a destination.

Ben Sweetland

I am the master of my fate;
I am the captain of my soul.

William E. Henley

There is only one success—to be able to spend your life in your own way.

Christopher Morley

If you can dream it, you can do it.

Walt Disney

There is a destiny that makes us brothers, none goes his way alone.
All that we send into the lives of others comes back into our own.

Edwin Markham

Knowing is not enough; we must apply. Willing is not enough; we must do.

Johann Wolfgang von Goethe

We grow great by dreams.

Woodrow Wilson

Without perseverance,
talent is a barren bed.

Welsh Proverb

Aim at the sun, and you may not reach it;
but your arrow will fly far higher
than if you aimed at an object
on a level with yourself.

J. Howse

Failure should challenge us
to new heights of **accomplishment**,
not pull us to new
depths of despair.
Failure is delay, but not defeat.
It is a temporary detour,
not a dead-end street.

William Arthur Ward

ACCOMPLISH

Webster's Collegiate Dictionary

Accomplish: 1. to bring to its goal or
                          conclusion
                   2. to carry out
                   3. to complete
                   4. to achieve

The Synonym Finder

Accomplish: perform, execute, carry out,
finish, polish off, expedite,
conclude, clinch, seal,
perfect, crown, produce,
consummate, bring about,
attain, arrive at, reach, win

People are always blaming their
circumstances for what they are.
I don't believe in circumstances.
The people who get on in this world are
they who get up and look for the
circumstances they want, and,
if they can't find them, make them.

George Bernard Shaw

Example is leadership.

Albert Schweitzer

I always prefer to believe the best
of everybody—it saves so much trouble.

Rudyard Kipling

Destiny is not a matter of chance,
it is a matter of choice;
it is not a thing to be waited for,
it is a thing to be achieved.

William Jennings Bryan

You do not get stomach ulcers
from what you eat. You get ulcers
from what is eating you.

Dr. Joseph F. Montague

It is a common experience
that a problem difficult at night
is resolved in the morning
after the committee of sleep
has worked on it.

John Steinbeck

Let us not bankrupt our todays
by paying interest on the regrets
of yesterday and by borrowing
in advance the troubles of tomorrow.

Ralph Sockman

Prior Preparation Prevents
Poor Performance.

Author Unknown

151

The quality of a person's life
is in direct proportion to their commitment
to excellence, regardless of their chosen
field of endeavor.

Vince Lombardi

Courage is the first of human
qualities because it is the
quality which guarantees all others.

Winston Churchill

In the battle of existence,
Talent is the punch;
Tact is the clever footwork.

Wilson Mizner

Have the courage to live.
Anyone can die.

Robert Cody

The best thing about the future
is that it comes only one day at a time.

Abraham Lincoln

It is better to be hated for what you are
than to be loved for what you are not.

Gide

Imagination
lit every lamp in this country,
produced every article we use,
built every church,
made every discovery,
performed every act
of kindness and progress,
created more and better things
for more people.
It is the priceless ingredient for a better day.

Henry J. Taylor

Strong **hope** is a much greater
stimulant of life
than any single realized joy
could be.

Friedrich Wilhelm Nietzsche

HOPE

Webster's Collegiate Dictionary

Hope: 1. the feeling that what is wanted can be had or that events will turn out for the best
2. a person or thing in which expectations are centered
3. to look forward to with desire and reasonable confidence
4. to want to believe

The Synonym Finder

Hope: expectation, desire, longing, want, anticipate, foresee, look forward, aspire, faith, trust, believe, feel confident, look on the bright side, security, optimism, conviction

Everyday, in every way,
I am getting better and better.

Emile Cove

One step by 100 persons is better than
100 steps by one person.

Koichi Tsukamoto

Put all good eggs in one basket
and then watch that basket.

Andrew Carnegie

The greatest thing in this world
is not so much where we are,
but in what direction we are moving.

Oliver Wendell Holmes

You may have to fight a battle
more than once to win it.

Margaret Thatcher

Always dream and shoot higher
than you know you can do.
Don't bother just to be better
than your contemporaries or predecessors.
Try to be better than yourself.

William Faulkner

One man with courage makes a majority.

Andrew Jackson

The world is full of cactus,
but we don't have to sit on it.

Will Foley

Keep your face to the sunshine
and you cannot see the shadows.

Helen Keller

Only a mediocre person is
always at his best.

Somerset Maugham

There is no verbal vitamin
more potent than praise.

Frederick B. Harris

Two men looked through prison bars—
One saw mud, the other stars.

Author unknown

The human mind, once stretched by a new idea, never regains its original dimensions.

Oliver Wendell Holmes

Lord, grant that I may always desire more than I can accomplish.

Michelangelo

Worse than a quitter is the man who is afraid to begin.

Author Unknown

Not failure, but low aim, is a crime.

Ernest Holmes

The most drastic
and usually the most effective
remedy
for fear is direct
action.

William Burnham

ACTION

Webster's Collegiate Dictionary

Action: 1. something done or performed
2. energetic activity
3. the state of being active
4. the effect produced on
something
5. the way of moving

The Synonym Finder

Action: movement, motion, effort,
endeavor, transaction, feat,
adventure, ways, vigor, vim,
energy, spirit, snap, effect,
result, practice, performance

The mind is its own place, and in itself can make a heaven of Hell, a hell of Heaven.

John Milton

Keep cool,
but do not freeze.

Author Unknown

If we all did the things
we are capable of doing,
we would literally astound ourselves.

Thomas Edison

An acre of performance is worth
a whole world of promise.

W.D. Howells

All you need in this life is ignorance and confidence, and then success is sure.

Mark Twain

The only thing we have to fear
is fear itself.

Franklin D. Roosevelt

If all our misfortunes were laid
in one common heap
whence everyone must take an
equal portion,
most people would be contented
to take their own and depart.

Socrates

The past, the present and the future are
really one—they are today.

Stowe

The block of granite
which was an obstacle
in the path of the weak,
becomes a stepping-stone
in the path of the strong.

Carlyle

The secret of success in life is for a
man to be ready for his
opportunity when it comes.

Benjamin Disraeli

Let us train our minds
to desire what the situation demands.

Seneca

When you can do the common things
of life in an uncommon way,
you will command the attention
of the world.

George Washington Carver

First things first, second things never.

Shirley Conran

We work not only to produce
but to give value to
time.

Eugene Delacroix

Our life is what our thoughts make it.

Marcus Aurelius

Our chief want in life is somebody
who will make us do what we can.

Ralph Waldo Emerson

There's no ceiling on
effort.

Harvey C. Fruehauf

EFFORT

Webster's Collegiate Dictionary

Effort: 1. exertion of physical or mental power
2. an earnest or strenuous attempt
3. an achievement
4. force or energy that is applied

The Synonym Finder

Effort: exertion, striving, struggle, application, grind, push, work, labor, toil, attempt, venture, endeavor, feat, achievement, attainment, aim, try

It is a fine thing to have ability, but the ability to discover ability in others is the true test.

Elbert Hubbard

A determined soul will do more
with a rusty monkey wrench
than a loafer will accomplish
with all the tools in a machine shop.

Rupert Hughes

I always view problems
as opportunities in work clothes.

Henry Kaiser

Who is more foolish,
the child afraid of the dark
or
the man afraid of the light?

Maurice Freehill

Failure is impossible.

Susan B. Anthony

Formula for failure:
Try to please everybody.

Herbert Bayard Swope

Only he who can see the invisible
can do the impossible.

Frank Gaines

We have to learn to be our own best
friends because we fall too easily into the
trap of being our worst enemies.

Roderick Thorp

To escape criticism—
do nothing, say nothing,
be nothing.

Elbert Hubbard

We are all here for a spell;
get all the good laughs you can.

Will Rogers

A man who wants to lead the orchestra
must turn his back on the crowd.

James Crook

Latent abilities are like clay.
It can be mud on shoes, brick in a building
or a statue that will inspire all who see it.
The clay is the same.
The result is dependent on how it is used.

James F. Lincoln

The best use of life is to spend it
for something that outlasts life.

William James

I shut my eyes in order to see.

Paul Gauguin

Never mind what others do;
do better than yourself,
beat your own record from day to day,
and you are a success.

William J. H. Boetcker

It is the spirit of a person
that hangs above him like a star in the sky.
People identify him at once, and join with
him until there is formed a parade of men
and women, thus inspired. No matter where
you find this spirit working, whether in a
person or an entire organization, you may
know that Heaven has dropped
a note of joy into the world.

George Matthew Adams

The human **spirit**
is stronger
than anything
that can happen to it.

C.C. Scott

SPIRIT

Webster's Collegiate Dictionary

Spirit: 1. activating or essential principle influencing a person
2. an inclination or impulse
3. a special attitude or frame of mind
4. enthusiastic loyalty
5. a lively or brisk quality in a person or his actions

The Synonym Finder

Spirit: heart, impulse, genius, quality, essence, truth, meaning, aim, humor, temperament, outlook, attitude, valor, courage, bravery, grit, vigor, daring, enthusiasm, eagerness, passion, energy, glow

I start where the last man left off.

Thomas A. Edison

If something goes wrong,
it is more important to talk about
who is going to fix it
than who is to blame.

Francis J. Gable

Life's greatest adventure is
in doing one's level best.

Arthur E. Morgan

When the best leader's work is done
the people say, "We did it ourselves."

Lao Tzu

Too many people are thinking of security
instead of opportunity.
They seem more afraid of life than death.

James F. Byrnes

You cannot run away from a weakness;
you must sometime fight it out or perish;
and if that be so, why not now,
and where you stand?

Robert Louis Stevenson

The measure of a man's real character
is what he would do if he knew
he never would be found out.

Thomas Babington Macaulay

To get profit without risk, experience
without danger, and reward without work,
is as impossible as it is to live
without being born.

A.P. Gouthey

No man is free
who is not
master
of his soul
and
controller
of his spirit.

Thomas Crombie

100
Motivational Idioms
That Should
Be in Bronze

Set the world on fire

Whistle in the dark

Actions speak louder than words

Early bird catches the worm

Gain ground

Nip it in the bud

Take a stand

Turn over a new leaf

Be as good as your word

Go like clockwork

Hitch your wagon to a star

Lead the way

Take by storm

Sprout wings

Run a tight ship

Work your fingers to the bone

To the nth degree

Bring to pass

Break the record

From the heart

Make up your mind

Hit the nail on the head

Keep your head above water

Buckle down

Carry the ball

Stand on your own feet

Let bygones be bygones

Leave no stone unturned

Keep plugging along

Break new ground

Dot the i's and cross the t's

Follow your heart

Have something on the ball

Get down to brass tacks

Turn the tables

Be worth your salt

Be ahead of the game

Better late than never

Bear down

Make a name for yourself

Know enough to come in out of the rain

Stand your ground

Burn the midnight oil

Get a jump on it

Win hands down

Put your best foot forward

Keep the ball rolling

Stick to your guns

Step on the gas

Have the guts to do something

Rise from the ashes

Set your sights

Put up or shut up

Speak the same language

Search your heart

Go through hell and high water

Be in the driver's seat

Be head and shoulders above

Earn your keep

Keep a stiff upper lip

Shape up or ship out

Make the grade

Mind your p's and q's

Be as cool as a cucumber

185

Put a feather in your cap

Feel like a million

Stand up and be counted

See beyond your nose

Run circles around it

Be the cream of the crop

Hit the books

Go down in history

Hit on all cylinders

Take your life in your hands

Cut the mustard

Square your shoulders

Stick your neck out

Be first and foremost

Keep your chin up

Get your foot in the door

Paddle your own canoe

Sit up and take notice

Take a crack at it

Come alive

Be fit as a fiddle

Read between the lines

Use elbow grease

Do first things first

Fish or cut bait

Take the bull by the horn

Think on your feet

Rock the boat

Keep your eye on the ball

Put your foot down

Raise the roof

Go out of your way

Don't let
the grass
grow under
your feet

See the
light
at the end
of the
tunnel

Every cloud
has
a
silver
lining

Carry the Torch

Subject Index

Kim D. Fellwock

4442 Mallard Point

Columbus, Indiana 47201

(812) 342-9773

www.fellwock.com